Pearls of Light

Codes and Messages from the Soul

Diane Dunn

Copyright © 2023 Diane Dunn. All rights reserved
ISBN: 9798399126272
Independently published

All artwork is the property of the author and may be shared with attribution.

Author photo by Yulia Kondyreva

Cover artwork: Diane Dunn
Cover design and book design: Wendy Crumpler www.wendycrumpler.com

Book and cover are set in Minion Pro

For Kiara, my soul
Thank you for your guidance and inspiration

For Yukia
Thank you for urging me to connect more deeply with
my soul and supporting me to do so.

For Wendy
Thank you for recognizing the universal wisdom in these
Pearls and making them into a book.

CONTENTS

Dedication	iii	Momentum	32	Free	70
Contents	v	Love	34	Sustenance	72
Introduction	vii	Tapestry	36	Integrity	74
Pearls & Codes	1	Wait	38	Dance	76
Grace	2	Peace	40	Stars	78
Change	4	Centered	42	Bright Side	80
Listening	6	Birth	44	Receive	82
Mystery	8	Pyramid	46	Research	84
Perspective	10	Nourishment	48	Roots	86
Equilibrium	12	Aware	50	Thrive	88
Faith	14	Wellspring	52	Ready	90
Willingness	16	Triggers	54	Transformation	92
Truth	18	Enthusiasm	56	Magic	94
Passenger	20	Orientation	58	Ease	96
Innovate	22	Bridge	60	Preparation	98
Sense of Humor	24	Signals	62	Risk	100
Pearls	26	Departure	64	Pot Luck	102
Soft Spot	28	Create	66	Symphony	104
Stillness	30	Trust	68	Flexible	106

Container	108	Consider	150	Implement	192
Divine Spark	110	Waves	152	Vulnerable	194
Capable	112	Compassion	154	Volunteer	196
Be Nimble	114	Wisdom	156	Harmony	198
Sacred Center	116	Unexpected	158	Expression	200
Relinquish Control	118	Meantime	160	Calm	202
Allow	120	Notice	162	Empowerment	204
Strength	122	Treasure Chest	164	Delightful	206
Synchronicity	124	Traveler of Light	166	Discernment	208
Express Yourself	126	Look Inside	168	Index of Pearls	210
In The Moment	128	Discomfort	170	About the Author	211
Befriend	130	Amethyst	172		
Refresh	132	Family	174		
Adapt	134	Discover	176		
Play	136	Rose	178		
Alchemy	138	Eyes	180		
Content	140	Receptive	182		
Reunion	142	Charm	184		
Surrender	144	Alignment	186		
Hands	146	Contrast	188		
Turtle & Eagle	148	Stability	190		

INTRODUCTION

In September 2022, I began a new practice communicating with my Soul, whose name is Kiara. We don't communicate with words, at least not words I understand with my logical mind. In order to better channel her advice, I sing and speak in a heart language I don't comprehend, freeing my mind to hear her more clearly.

It's a liberating daily practice that has taught me to trust my inner knowing and connection with soul-wisdom. After singing and speaking in this Light language, I draw a code using color markers, chosen by inspiration. The codes are equally inspired, shaped without thought. It's only then I write down what I understand her message to be.

The practice has shifted over the months since I began. Sometimes I hear a word just before waking or while I am meditating in my morning bath. The word becomes a focus and the message unfolds. Other times, I pick up my pen without a thought to what the message might be and let the words appear. It is amazing to me how often the Pearl is so timely related to something that happens only later in the day, offering assistance I was yet aware I needed.

This practice has opened me to hear and see and expand beyond what I had formerly known. I use two different apps to enhance the colors and texture of my handwritten codes, which for me has been a new venture into creative technology. My communication with Kiara has deepened with practice as have her pearls of wisdom and light.

Friends who read my daily posts have commented to me how the Pearl and the code seem to be speaking directly to them about issues in their own lives. I have come to realize these messages, although personal to me, can be helpful to you as well.

Each morning you can flip through the book intuitively stopping on a page to read your message and meditate on the code. Or you can start at the beginning, reading as many as you would like to inspire your day.

I also encourage you to do the same practice I have been doing, connecting with your soul by singing and speaking a language that is not from your logical mind. Then, draw a code with colored markers and write in your journal what your heart is communicating to you through your soul.

The apps I use are PIXLR and LUNAPIC which can be downloaded for free.

May PEARLS OF LIGHT inspire you to more deeply connect with the unseen world assisting you at every turn.

PEARLS & CODES

GRACE

There is no resource available more healing than love. The frequency, the vibration of love can be sprinkled like grace-filled fairy dust on yourself and everyone around you. It flows abundantly from the divine for you to partake. Share it today with everyone you encounter. Grace heals both the giver and receiver.

Grace

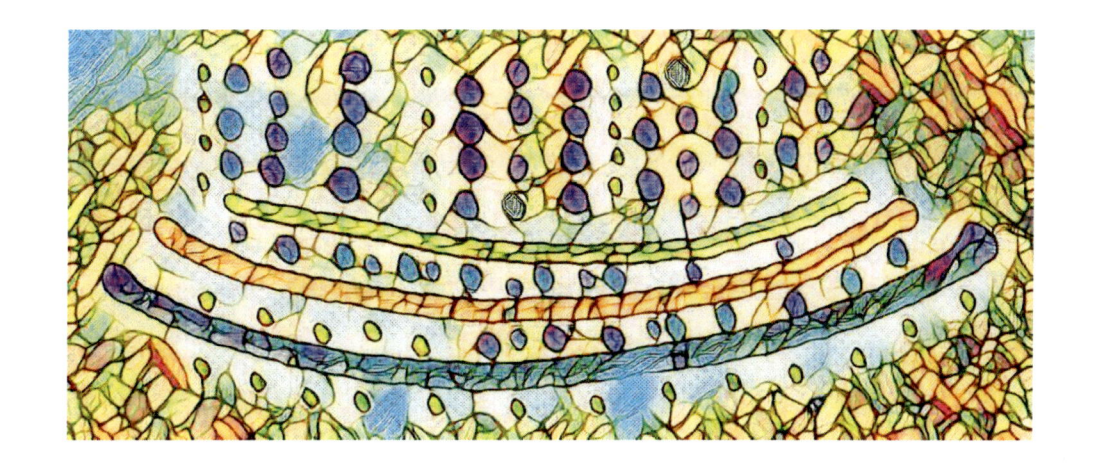

CHANGE

To participate in change, begin with altering your daily routine. Even just a small change indicates to the universe your commitment to creating change on a grander scale, instead of waiting for it to happen. As you disperse your resistance to keeping things the same, the energy field around you shifts and the change you are looking for is activated.

Change

LISTENING

When you feel blocked—struggling to release the heavy emotions gripping you—the loving listening ear of a friend can work magic. You exist in an intricate web of energy where balance is necessary for the whole to function well. Sometimes you are the one who holds space, allowing the other to shift and release. Other times you are assisted by a friend to alter your energy field, coming back to your center. Give thanks for this network of love and light, where being present and listening can bring healing and relief.

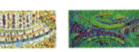

Listening

MYSTERY

You have arrived at the place of unknown potential, where everything is created but not yet in form. It requires you to trust the magic is unfolding in your life, even if you cannot see it. At such a time, draw on the wisdom of your instinct. Delve deep to honor the receptive side of your nature, where unknowable forces are working in your life. Let the mystery flow.

Mystery

PERSPECTIVE

Not everything you think is pointing a certain way turns out to be so. Look at it from a different perspective. Something better than you thought could be on the way. Allow yourself a broader vision. From above and beyond, the small things fall away and the bigger picture emerges. The details are less important. Continue to trust in life's unfolding even when it's not how you envisioned it.

Perspective

EQUILIBRIUM

Finding balance between being comfortable and functioning outside your comfort zone is an exercise in equilibrium. The composure you seek is not in one or the other but how they interplay with each other, finding comfort in the uncomfortable, finding creativity in the static, finding stability in the unstable. Seek equilibrium in all the nooks and crannies where imbalance may be lurking.

Equilibrium

FAITH

When calling in what you want to manifest, it is important you have faith in your own clarity and trust there are unseen forces in the universe conspiring to assist what is for your highest good. You may doubt your own power to create miracles, but miracles are gifts freely given with no need for you to do anything except graciously receive them. Have faith that what you're waiting for is on its way.

Faith

WILLINGNESS

To move into the unknown, all you need is willingness, with trust in your pocket and compassion in your heart. As you stand in front of the doors to rooms you have yet to explore, know you are surrounded by the love of your guides and angels even though you walk alone in a passageway that seems dark. Be willing and the universe will light your way.

Willingness

TRUTH

When something rings true for you, go a little deeper to question why. Then hold it in your heart and see if it continues to shine and resonate with what you know is so. Use these stored inner truths to inform the choices and decisions you make, to support and empower your actions. With so much information floating through the airwaves, self-discovery is a process worth engaging.

Truth

PASSENGER

The anticipation you are feeling is a worthy vehicle for your plans to progress. The energy is accelerating. Your team is coming together, fulfilling your intentions. Trust the momentum to drive itself. Become a passenger without directing the destination. Enjoy the ride.

Passenger

INNOVATE

Now is the time for innovation—to creatively redefine yourself. Examine and release what was but is no more. Innovatively name who you are now and the direction you are moving. Innovation allows you to observe yourself from new angles and creative perspectives. This viewpoint initiates movement on your path of discovery. Innovate.

Innovate

SENSE OF HUMOR

Sometimes circumstances become so bizarre you just have to laugh, because pulling your hair out isn't worth the pain. Screaming at the top of your lungs is another option, but not as satisfying in the end as a deep and sincere belly laugh. When magical beauty mixes with nerve-racking blockages and frustrating detours, best to observe the experience as a comedy of errors where somehow it all works out in the end. A good sense of humor is required.

Sense of Humor

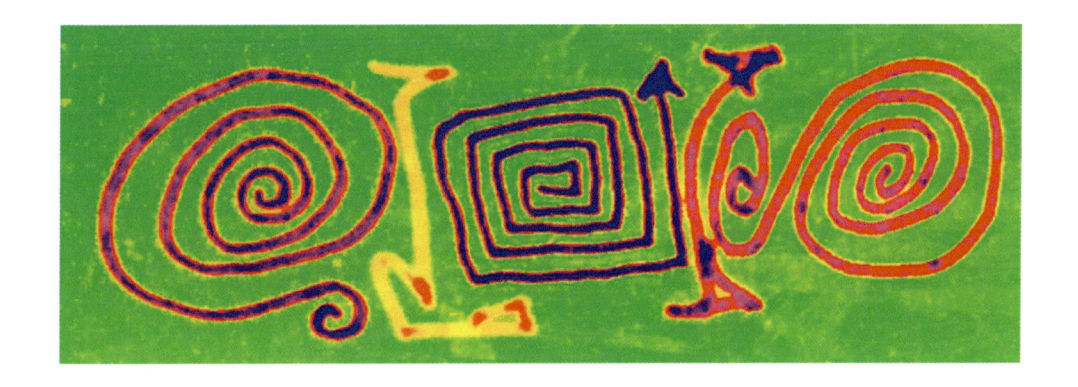

PEARLS

Do you know how pearls are made? When an irritant particle becomes trapped in a mollusk, it coats the irritant with mother of pearl, protecting its soft vulnerable body from discomfort. It's a lovely metaphor for transforming your own irritants into precious gems. You can coat the things that irritate you with softness until the aggravation is no longer abrasive. Then you can look at it in a different way, seeing the chance for it to teach you something new about yourself and grow. Each pearl you create this way represents a valuable lesson for how to shift your troubles into treasures.

Pearls

SOFT SPOT

Being in the flow with creation itself offers support and propulsion, moving you on your path with effortless ease. Find that soft spot and step into it. Feel the charge, like a beam of light shining your way forward. Float in it, trusting you are being taken in an exciting new direction.

Soft Spot

STILLNESS

Be still, for in the stillness you can hear the secrets whispered in the wind. You can recognize the luminescence of life and rest in its glow. In the stillness, you become the receptacle of jewels from Divine Source and can translate the sound of silence in which mystical wisdom resides. Be still and you will receive what your heart is longing to know.

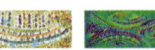

Stillness

MOMENTUM

After pondering, reflecting, resisting and releasing, comes movement, where you experience the pieces of the puzzle coming together and the picture coming into focus. A new phase has begun. Feel the excitement and anticipation but know the work now springs into action. Keep the momentum moving.

Momentum

LOVE

Swim in a pool of love today. Let it soothe and relax you. Feel it flowing around you, through you, in you. There is no greater healing frequency than Love. Float in it. Splash it around. Today, swim in a pool of love.

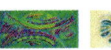

———————————————   Love   ———————————————

35

TAPESTRY

You are part of a cosmic soul family who connect and reconnect in each lifetime. Some you know well, some you are yet to encounter or meet in special moments. When you reunite, there is a golden light that shines, reminding you of the colorful luminous threads that form the tapestry of your ancient tribe whose purpose is to illuminate hope and love where darkness and obscurity sometimes hold sway. As you gather and your hearts touch, joy reigns.

Tapestry

WAIT

There are days for making decisions and taking action but today is not one of them. Wait for the confluence to appear. Wait for the fruit to ripen. Sometimes a delay is beneficial for things to develop in a deeper way. Be present to what is evolving without being overly eager for the outcome. Then, the waiting can be enjoyed.

Wait

PEACE

Peace begins in your conscious imagination. Look for it. See it. Act from it. When you can see the whole unseparated, union with the Divine can assist you. Humanity was created as parts of a united whole. To be at war with any of the parts is self-destructive. Awaken to the truth of your unity, then peace is possible in your lifetime. Begin with yourself.

Peace

CENTERED

When life is shifting and reforming, it is important to stay centered with your reactions and responses. Like the teeter-totter you played on as a child, sitting on the edge of the plank, the ups and downs are substantial. In the middle, you can feel the movement without the extremes. When you ground yourself on the earth, you can remain centered even as life has you stretching beyond your comfort zone.

Centered

BIRTH

Your gestation period is coming to fruition. The linkages inside you and in the material realm are coming together and about to bear fruit. The divine wellspring feeding your intention has brought forth the pathway for delivery. Feel the shift and sense the excitement. Your new project is about to be born.

Birth

PYRAMID

There are some people who have weak or non-existent boundaries around them, so their energies and emotions spill out onto those in their proximity. To protect yourself from any heavy energies in your environment, it's important to strengthen the luminous grid around you each morning by visualizing a pyramid of light above the top of your head, reaching down below your feet, anchored firmly in the earth. As you see it, recite several affirmations such as: "I am love. I am strong. I am compassionate." Then close the pyramid around you by saying three times: "I know who I am. I am safe and secure." This practice will keep your own energy field strong and wide.

Pyramid

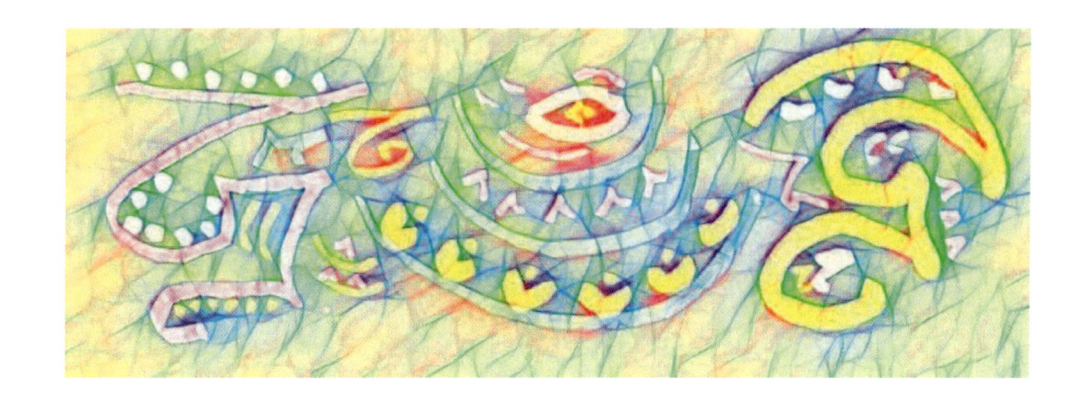

NOURISHMENT

At times when things are shifting, it is important to nourish yourself, both your body and your soul. Be conscious of what feeds you—movement, color, taste. Avoid consuming what make you feel heavy and flat. Nourishment comes in many forms. Choose what enlivens you, what is health-giving, growth-filled and wholesome. Nourish yourself.

Nourishment

AWARE

Be aware today—of what you're feeling, of what you are putting out into the world. Your attitude determines what you experience, what is reflected back to you. Have an awareness of what you encounter around you and how you respond. Be the observer. Imagine you have a magic wand and you are conducting an orchestra with it. Make beautiful music.

Aware

WELLSPRING

You were created with a wellspring of opportunities for discovery and exploration. Look deep within yourself today for this bountiful source. Pause there to recognize what you have been seeking. Give thanks for it. Contemplate how you can live differently having identified this treasure. Claim it as your own.

Wellspring

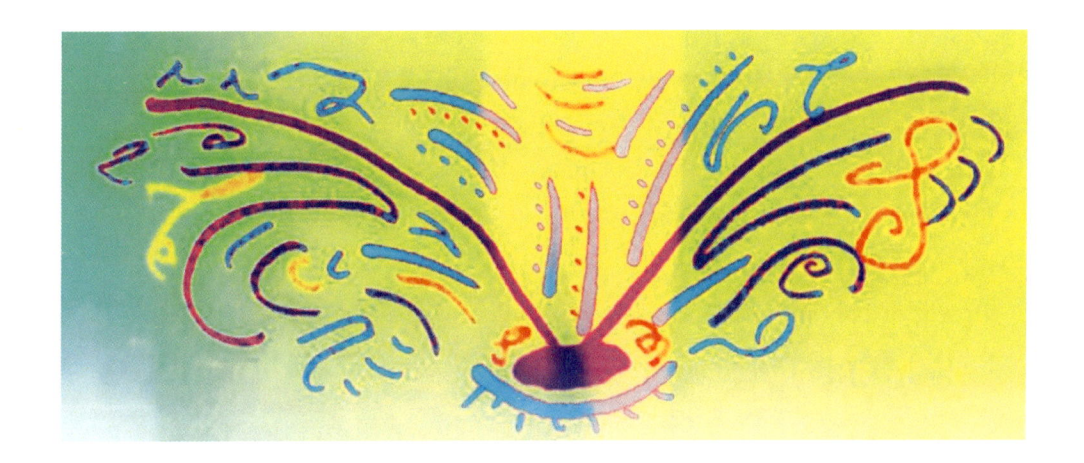

TRIGGERS

Trying to fix or change someone else is folly and will only lead to frustration. Asking yourself why you have that impulse will help you identify what the person is triggering in you. When you feel discomfort or irritation, imagine the other is holding up a mirror for you to look at yourself and your desire to correct what you see as wrong or problematic. Turn your attention from the one you want to fix, to yourself. Feel what you are feeling. Hold the feeling in your hands and observe it with compassion and awareness. This is the path of self-care. Honor your process.

Triggers

ENTHUSIASM

Be enthusiastic today—even for just an hour. Enthusiasm is the fuel that recharges your inner battery with joy for life. Choose something to do that makes your heart sing—have lunch or tea with a friend, dance to an oldie you loved in your youth, play with paint, splashing color on a page. The outcome isn't important. It's the manner of doing it that matters. Being enthusiastic is a choice you can make.

———————————————   Enthusiasm   ———————————————

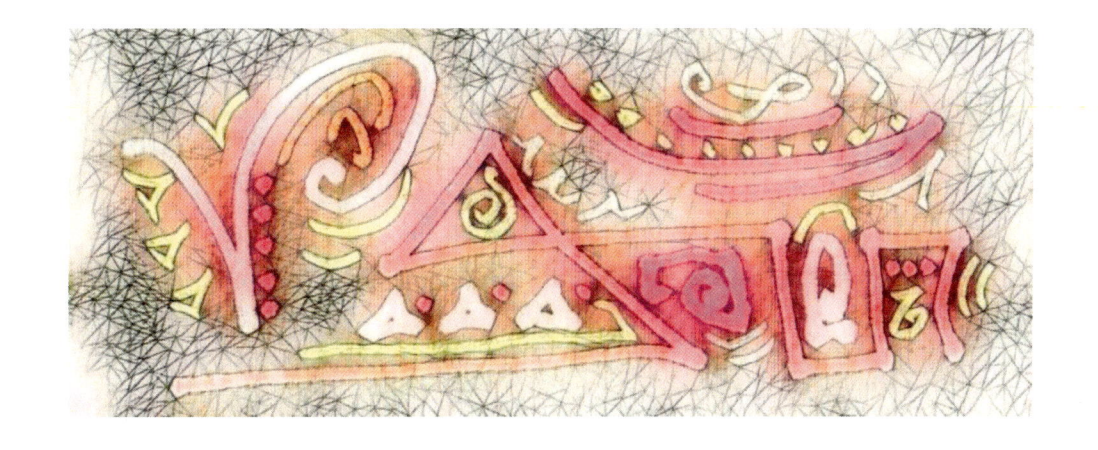

ORIENTATION

Today is orientation for the new terraine you find yourself in, over and beyond the rainbow. The language is different. To learn it well, listen to the birds singing, the dogs barking, the rooster crowing. The sounds are coded. You can locate yourself inside of them and begin to sense the meaning. It's beautiful here. Find your place in it and sing with joy for you have arrived home.

Orientation

BRIDGE

Be the bridge that connects people from the shadow to the sunshine, from the obscure to clarity, from frustration to peace, from loneliness to unity. Make your bridge beautiful with flowers and sweet-smelling herbs so people are invited to investigate what's on the other side; so they will cross from the ordinary to the amazing. Be the bridge.

Bridge

SIGNALS

A subtle type of attention is needed to receive the signals and messages coming your way. When circumstances take you off your direct path or pattern, look for the insight or opportunity to see things differently. A detour can signal a shift in your life. Seeds can be planted for new growth to occur. Pay attention to these signals. They are pregnant with possibilities.

Signals

DEPARTURE

Today begins a new adventure, a departure from the ordinary. Smile. Trust. Rest in the truth that you are being led, guided, surrounded by the light, lifted up and held in the palm of divine grace. Whatever happens is part of the adventure. Delight in the mystery of it.

Departure

CREATE

By doing something freeform and creative every day, you balance the hemispheres of your brain: draw with your eyes closed; paint with your non-dominant hand; dance around the room to your favorite music; sing with lyrics you make up as you go, to a tune of your own design; lie on your back in the grass cloud-gazing, seeing animals and giants and castles form and fade. These creative practices expand your consciousness and tickle your soul.

Create

TRUST

Trust is a present-moment practice. Logic tells you there is no way for you to control what happens but relinquishing the idea of control takes conscious practice. Stress and anxiety render you blind to the opportunities offered in the present moment. Trust releases doubt and worry and illuminates life's gifts available to you only in the here and now. Practice trust and see what life offers you today (and tomorrow too!).

Trust

FREE

Freedom is a sensibility related to movement, peace, and tranquility. Liberate yourself from the inside out. Break free from notions that contain you, that restrict your creativity, so new ideas can awaken within you. Set free constricting reality and be an agent for change. Be how you were born to be.

———————————————   Free   ———————————————

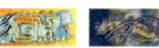

SUSTENANCE

Draw sustenance for your inner core—not just your body—for your whole being cannot be sated by food and drink alone. Divine inspiration comes to you in many forms, especially in nature. Feeding your spirit, you are sustained by the wisdom and enduring support of that which is beyond the frailty of material limitations. Sustenance for your core, empowers confidence and faith to accomplish your goals.

Sustenance

INTEGRITY

'To thine own self be true' sometimes feels as complicated as a jigsaw puzzle. Start with the things about yourself you know are so: your physical traits, your location, your passions and concerns. These form the edges of your truth, the borders. Then in the center put the pieces you know but sometimes doubt; angels and other unseen light beings offer you guidance and protection. If you ask them, they will complete your puzzle. Being true to yourself, it will follow as the night, the day, you won't be false to any other. That is integrity.

Integrity

DANCE

A wonderful way to shift energy and lift your spirits is to dance. Moving to music that resonates with your heart center, sends waves of light through your physical body and radiates out, creating a wide auric field those around you can also feel. Dance today to your own inner song or with the music blaring. Dance.

Dance

STARS

When you are blessed to view the night sky before the moon rises and there are nearly no lights of human making, you see the majesty of the cosmos fill the sky. Is there anything more magnificent? You begin to understand your place in this breathtaking reality, knowing you have a purpose to bring down this divine light into the world. Let it shine so others can feel it and remember who they really are. Shine like the stars.

Stars

BRIGHT SIDE

Many people are doing good in the world, in small and grand ways. There are also the ones who do disturbing destructive things for questionable reasons. Focusing on the bright side does not deny the shadow but rather creates more light. It encourages you to add to the goodness, to find ways to contribute to positive change. Your attention to the virtuous brings out of hiding those who want to augment the light. Be mindful where you put your energy. Better to look on the bright side.

Bright Side

RECEIVE

Each day has something new to offer you if you are looking. The more attentive you are moment to moment, the more you will see, the more you will notice, the more you will receive. Go outside, look at the sky, touch the ground. Then put your hands on your heart center. You are part of creation. Receive what the day is offering you.

Receive

RESEARCH

Explore what interests you by searching for others who are interested in the same thing. Research what is already happening in the world and see if it fits with what feels right for you. Seek out new and creative ways to develop and generate concepts and understanding to move your ideas forward. Research is your starting point.

Research

ROOTS

When a seed is planted, the first thing to grow are the roots, anchored into the ground providing nourishment for the plant to flourish and bear fruit. Your roots are what offer you stability and support. They are the source of your vital energy. Be conscious how you walk today. Feel your foot touch the ground, lift off and touch the ground again. This secure connection with the earth assists you to thrive and bloom.

Roots

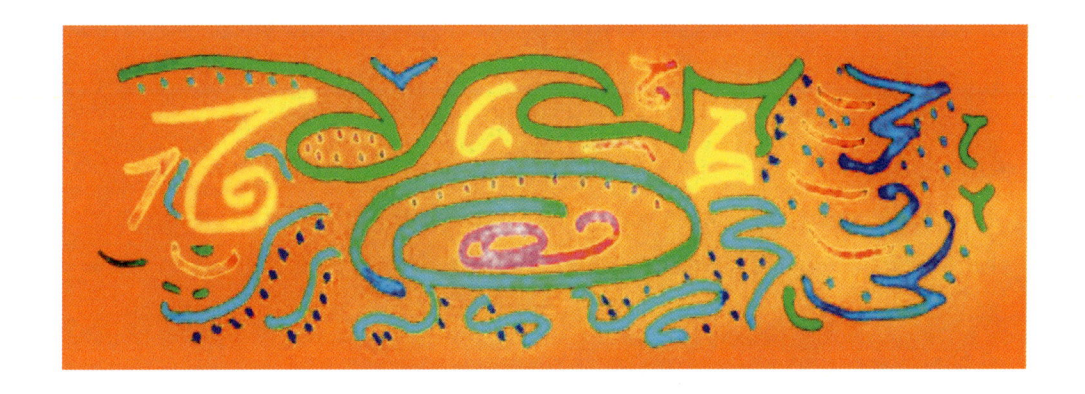

THRIVE

Whether the sun is shining or the clouds obscure its rays, life continues to thrive. You grow and prosper from the heart of who you are. Perhaps the movement is slower than you'd hoped but remember your intentions have their own rhythm, flourishing in their own way. Focus on the process and watch the mission reveal itself. Watch it thrive.

Thrive

READY

When life seems to be working in your favor, be grateful and reflect. Your readiness allows for life to work on your behalf. When you release your doubts and the obstacles fall away, you are reclaiming your power to perform for your highest good and the good of others. Bless what has gone before as you let it go, for all of what has brought you here. You are ready for what lies ahead.

Ready

TRANSFORMATION

Transformation isn't as hard as you might think. Start by converting your heavy energy into light, with the help of Pachamama and your intention. Soften what is hard, loosen what is tight. Recall what irritation feels like in your body, the tension it creates, and what happens when you turn your scowl into a smile. That's transformation. The more you practice it, the better prepared you will be when the opportunity for grander transformation presents itself.

Transformation

MAGIC

When you tap into the energy of the mountains, the ocean, the forest or a rocky stream, you are connecting to the magic of life. They say magicians can influence the course of events in mysterious and supernatural ways. But there is nothing more natural than using the power and frequency of the elements and nature to assist you in creating and manifesting your conscious intentions. Try it. Discover the magic.

Magic

95

EASE

Ease is a choice—not to make everything easy because sometimes the current of life is rough—but when you choose to be in the flow, you claim assistance from divine source. Imagine a river. You can choose to go in the direction of the current or hold on to a rock in an effort to stay where you are, barely keeping your head above water. Trying to stay put, you will be tossed and battered. Choosing to let the current take you, requires you to trust where you are headed is a better place than standing still or fighting against where life is taking you. By choosing ease over struggle, you will be guided on your path.

Ease

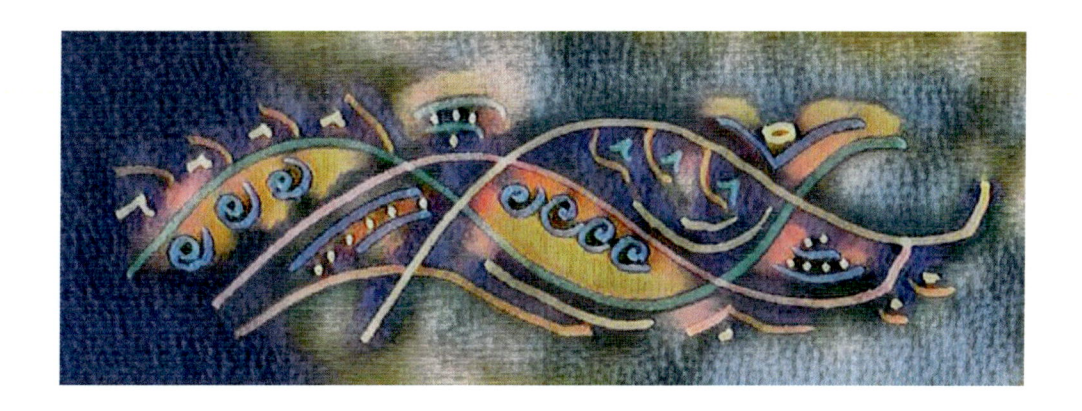

PREPARATION

There are practical things you can do to prepare for trips, travel, transition, shifts. But the most important thing you can do is be present in the moment. Be light on your feet and trust your first impulse on how to respond to the circumstances you find yourself in. The best preparation, with eyes wide open, is an open heart.

Preparation

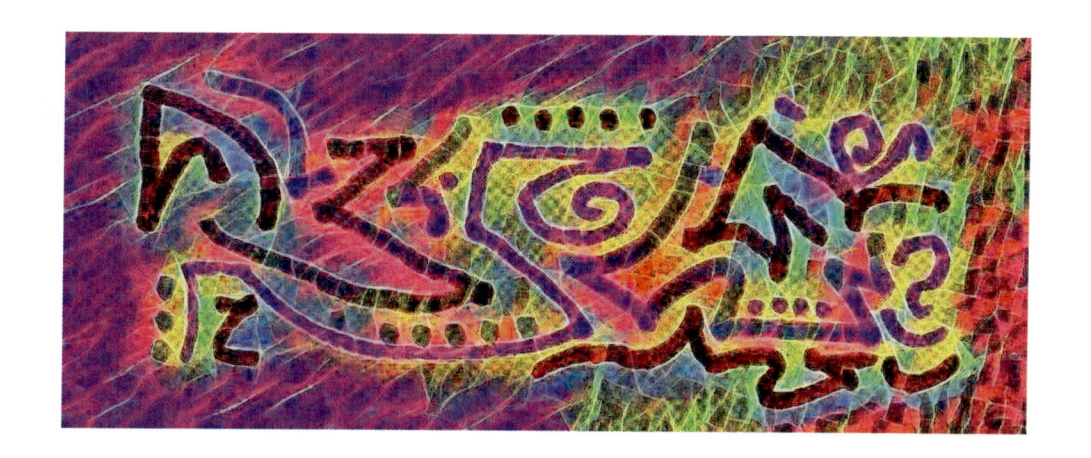

RISK

Manifesting your desires involves risk, embracing the unknown for the promise of what it can bring. When you risk taking action that is uncertain and feels precarious, you can tap into the magic of life that doesn't exist in the safety zone. Your dreams can become reality if you are willing to move beyond your fear. Take a risk. See what happens.

Risk

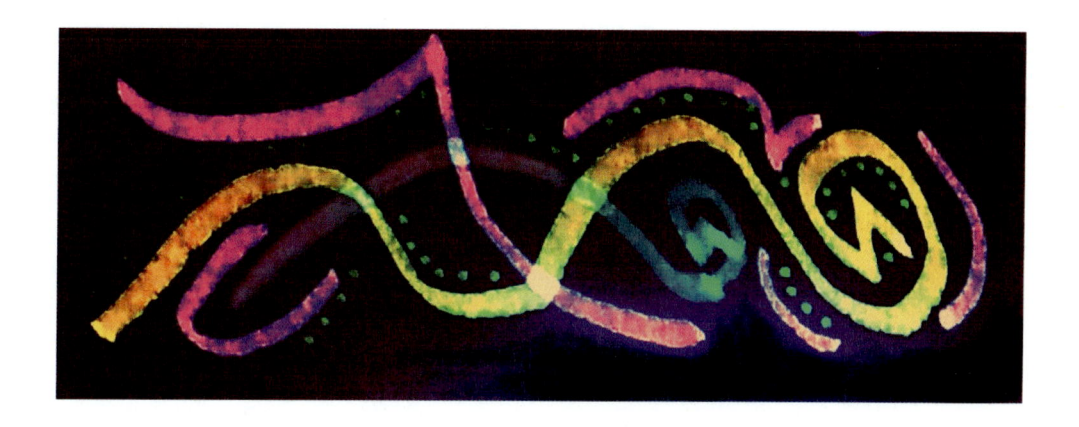

POT LUCK

When friends and neighbors get together for a pot luck meal, a delightful assortment of specialties are shared. It's a perfect metaphor for life in community where each one contributes their gifts and abilities without plan or judgement, creating a whole that is more than the sum of its parts. Bring your uniqueness to the table, trusting others to do the same.

Pot Luck

SYMPHONY

Living life well is like conducting a symphony. Sometimes the horn section dominates or the violins. Each movement has its own tempo and tone. The trick is to harmonize and balance each crescendo, each allegro, each adagio. Conduct the symphony of your life with gusto, making all the music resplendent.

Symphony

FLEXIBLE

Life is full of surprises, twists and turns, with unexpected interruptions and detours. By remaining flexible, you can navigate whatever the day brings your way. Make intentions without expectations for how they come to pass. Every day can be a new adventure. Enjoy the exploration of it.

Flexible

CONTAINER

In childhood development, toddlers need safe containers from which they can push against boundaries. The children learn to negotiate limits, moving beyond them into freedom but not so far that they get lost, unable to find the way back to the familiar safe space. As an adult, you also push the boundaries of your safe container to explore new possibilities and to expand your horizons, which is heathy. Yet there are still times when finding your way back to what's comfortable and familiar, can serve you, allowing for integration of all you are discovering. The safety zone is not where you stay but some days it's helpful to find shelter there.

Container

DIVINE SPARK

As humans, you have a base instinct for survival but you also have within you the spark of divinity that urges you beyond survival. Your divine aspect longs for empathetic, altruistic connection with others. Nurture this impulse. It is the source of your internal power and renders you capable of creating a world where peace and harmony thrive.

Divine Spark

CAPABLE

You have the capacity to transform visions into reality. By contemplating the vision you want to manifest, ideas start to come. Then, step by step, the building blocks form and take shape. The projects have been different but the process is more or less the same. You are capable of creating the world the way you want it to be. Let the ideas flow.

Capable

BE NIMBLE

A situation you thought was ideal, turned out not to be. It's distressing, I know. However, when something comes to an end, new circumstances emerge. You can fret that the new state of affairs won't be as good as what it is replacing or you can imagine what is evolving will be even better than what was. Now is a time when everything you've taken for granted is up for grabs. Be nimble, light on your feet, with trust in your heart. Then, what unfolds could be a joyful surprise.

Be Nimble

SACRED CENTER

Whenever you find yourself in the midst of disruption, breathe deeply to enter a peaceful place inside yourself. Peace is located in your sacred center even when chaos reigns around you. Breathe and smile, remembering that place exists. Visualize a beam of light entering your crown and send the light out through your heart center into the world. This will not only calm you, it will shift the frequency around you as well.

Sacred Center

RELINQUISH CONTROL

There is a difference between trying to control outside circumstances and consciously choosing how to respond to them. You can choose to comfort and care for yourself. You can choose to protect yourself by walking away. You can choose to seek out a friend for assistance. By releasing any effort to control the behavior of another, you claim confidence in your ability to choose what's best for you.

Relinquish Control

ALLOW

Whether life is flowing smoothly or you are facing challenges, if you allow the moment free passage, you will be guided by a power beyond your own. When you allow, you are trusting there is a creative force working on your behalf. Your energy can sync with it and, like wind catching a sail, you can move through the waves with ease and grace, allowing life to unfold.

Allow

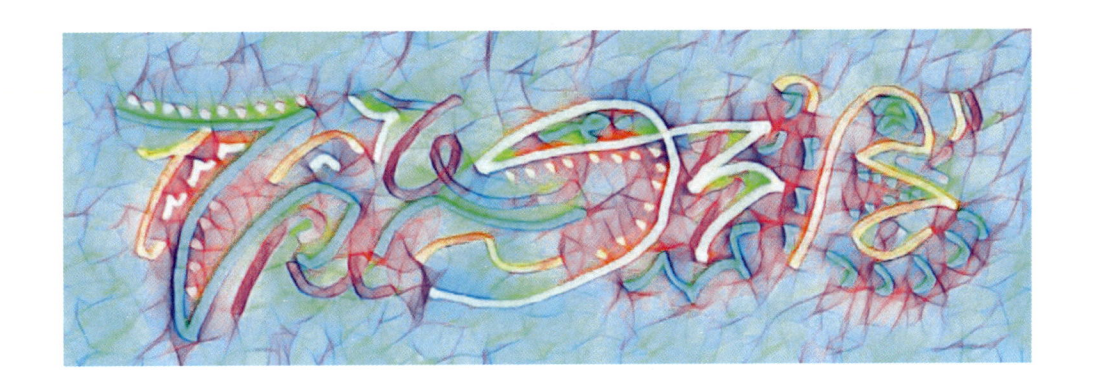

STRENGTH

Vital strength is the strength it takes to be fully alive. To be able to say, "I am here. I am capable, I am courageous, I am compelled to reveal my heart's desires and bring them into form. Use this vital strength so your life is expressive and meaningful.

——————————————— Strength ———————————————

SYNCHRONICITY

It may seem the events of life are random but there is an energetic flow that has meaning and purpose if you can tune in to the frequency of the grand conductor. Pay attention to the little things that connect you on your path of exploration. Surprising coincidence always has a message beyond the obvious. Be a conscious observer and you will see the assistance being offered to you around every corner.

Synchronicity

EXPRESS YOURSELF

Creative self-expression—drawing, dancing, singing, writing, cooking—opens your intuition and quiets the limiting beliefs of the mind. While you are waiting for your next steps to clarify, express yourself through movement, sound, color and taste. These acts will connect you with the source of creation where all new projects and ideas are conceived. Express yourself.

Express Yourself

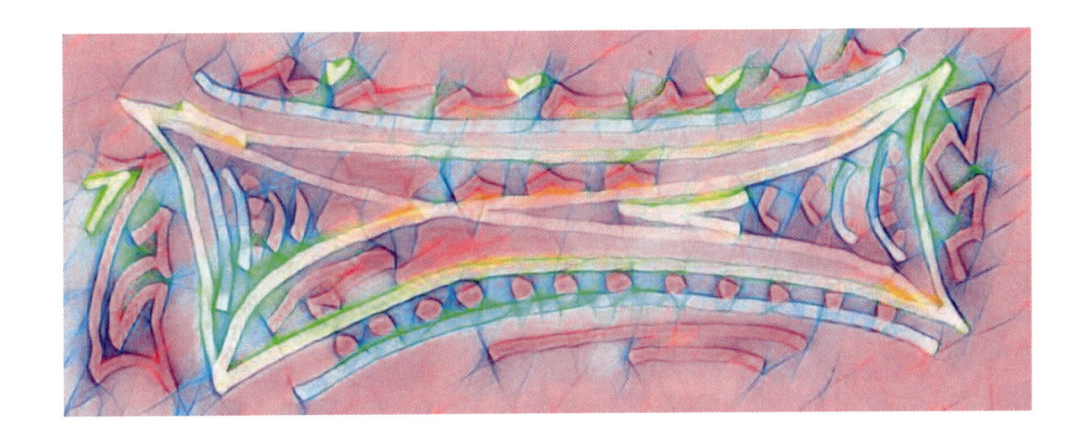

IN THE MOMENT

Being present in each moment allows you to savor the experiences as they are happening, especially the encounters you have with other people. Being in the moment prevents you from assuming or projecting what you think you already know, amplifying your awareness. Spontaneity blossoms, happiness flows, pleasure flourishes.

In the Moment

BEFRIEND

By befriending people different from yourself, you expand your horizon, connecting to a network of light for the planetary shift that is approaching. The coming together of a variety of cultures, backgrounds, and life experiences offers a pool of resources for playfully engaging in the development of new energetic systems. Be open to that which you don't already know. Create opportunities to move beyond the familiar to discover both differences and what unites you as humanity.

Befriend

REFRESH

It's a new day. Hit the reset button. Release yesterday and before, to the land of Has Been. Don't hunt for hassles. Refresh your body and mind. Dance your cells awake to recognize the possibilities today presents. Allow life to enchant you. Reinvigorate. Revitalize. Refresh.

Refresh

ADAPT

A wonderful tool to use when things don't seem to be going your way, is adaptability. When you can adapt yourself to whatever might be happening around you, you have the ability to see another way, other possibilities. Life offers an endless supply of opportunities for growth and expansion. By adapting to your current circumstances, you are empowered to create alternatives.

Adapt

PLAY

Life is a playground. You can do calisthenics led by the man in charge or you can go exploring. Discover hidden cave drawings. Dig for buried treasure, finding ancient wisdom. Scavenge for covert messages. Fly with birds and butterflies, amplifying your awareness. Expose secret mysteries. Even if you're working, find a way to play, using your imagination to create the world you want. Life is a playground. Investigate its magic.

Play

ALCHEMY

The art of alchemy is discovering what nature knows innately—the transformation of what is base into something pure and radiant. Practicing this art, you can learn to transform base emotions, like blame and judgement, into refined energy to build new attitudes and systems promoting peace, light, and love. Connect with Nature and she will teach you. Practice alchemy to discover the magic of life.

Alchemy

CONTENT

What does it take for you to be content? Is it when you balance your time communing in nature with taking care of 'biz'? Is it when you spend time alone as well as time with others? Is it when you contemplate and reflect in a balanced way with being active? Finding the right recipe is a fluid thing so pay attention to your feelings as you are feeling them. It will help you locate your centered place where contentment resides.

Content

REUNION

Souls reincarnate in clusters which means significant people in your life have probably been significant to you in previous lives. There are ones you agreed to meet again to complete something unfinished and there are others you loved so dearly you long to reconnect. These soul reunions can be brief or lengthy but they are always deep and meaningful connections. Be on the lookout for a special reunion coming your way.

Reunion

SURRENDER

No matter what the outside circumstance, contentment is always an inside job. It begins with accepting what is. When something happens that shocks or upsets you, it's difficult because you wanted and expected it would be different. The effort to change what is, however, will be a losing battle. Rather, surrender to it. Breathe. Let go. From that point of peace, you can better choose how to respond. From that place of acceptance, you can recognize options not visible in your state of battle. No need to feel weak or defeated, the surrender is empowering, even satisfying. Embrace what is happening in the moment and contentment will naturally follow.

Surrender

HANDS

Sometimes you need a helping hand—with your luggage, with your life. And sometimes you can give one. A drop of love is given and received in each exchange. These drops can fill an ocean, making the world a better place, one hand at a time. Participate.

Hands

TURTLE & EAGLE

Your energy field and scope are expanding. As you move into a new cycle, call on the spirit of the eagle and the turtle. One allows your focus to be expansive. The other keeps you grounded and confident. These totems connect you with both the Air element and the Earth—amplification and transformation. These two guardians are assisting you with the transition you are undergoing. They both are fearless and travel light. Trust in their guidance.

Turtle & Eagle

CONSIDER

The energy of the cosmos is speaking with you. Take time to consider these messages even if you don't understand them with your logical mind. Notice the small encounters you have with people that happen unexpectedly. An overheard conversation between others could also be relevant for you. Consideration is called for. Listen carefully.

Consider

WAVES

Life is rarely static. It moves in waves—ups and downs, ins and outs, highs and lows. The waves can be a gentle pulse like those in a cove or, as during inclement weather on the open sea, the waves can be deep and daunting. When life feels stormy, it's time to lay low, finding shelter inside yourself. Use this inward motion to examine what really matters to you, what you want to create, and what you want to release. When the sun returns and the current is calm again, you can float with ease, confident in which direction you want to go.

Waves

COMPASSION

It's a softening of your heart. In a world with so many sharp edges and harsh words, it's important to smooth out the scratchy fabric of life rather than contributing to its roughness. Compassion is key to creating an atmosphere where transformation can be fostered— your own and the world's. Soften your heart.

Compassion

WISDOM

Hidden inside you is a chamber of mysteries waiting for you to find it. The path of discovery cannot be accessed with your conscious mind, for it is too small to hold this ancient and timeless wisdom. Rather look with your intuition and perception in deep meditation, in your quiet time and your dream time. This code is the key to enter the chamber of sacred wisdom. Use it well.

Wisdom

157

UNEXPECTED

When the unexpected happens, welcome it in. Allow the surprise to take shape and become what it will. When things go the way you expect, you are in your comfort zone. Respond to the unexpected as an opportunity to interrupt your routine. Enjoy the adventure to navigate the new, to see what it can teach you. The unexpected keeps you on your toes.

Unexpected

MEANTIME

Sometimes it seems like you are waiting around for the main event of your life to begin. But in the meantime, there are interesting things happening all around you. Listen to the raindrops landing on your windowpane, to the whistle of your boiling kettle as you prepare your tea. Notice the numbers on the clock when you pick up your phone and the background color of the ad flashing on your computer screen. There are messages and clues for you to discover and decipher. The main event of your life is now.

Meantime

NOTICE

It may seem like an ordinary day. Raindrops fall on the parched earth and the plants rejoice. Birds sing their happy songs. But from the cosmic perspective, nothing is ordinary. Shifts and changes are happening everywhere. Notice how your body feels. Be aware of your emotions—when and where. Tune in to the vibration of your energy field calibrating with the frequencies coming down from the sun. Notice.

Notice

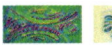

TREASURE CHEST

Create your own treasure chest by putting inside the things you value about yourself. Be specific. Then add the special moments you have shared with others. There is lots of room. Then recall moments of transcendent magic with nature and the divine. Give them a special spot inside. See the luster and sparkle you have created in your treasure chest. Register the way you feel looking at it all. Then close the lid but know you can open it whenever the need arises, to remind you how remarkable your life is.

Treasure Chest

TRAVELER OF LIGHT

Think of yourself as a traveler of Light who came to this planet at this time to shine brightly. Even though sometimes you forget who you really are and why you came, your heart and soul remember. Hold that image today, of yourself as a being of Light, traveling on a mission to bring the vibration of love and unity with all your fellow travelers.

Traveler of Light

LOOK INSIDE

Your tendency is to look to the outside world for the change you seek. Instead, look inside yourself where the seed of your new project is germinating. Nourish its growth there and soon it will be your outside focus as well, the birth of which will happen in its time. Don't try to push the river. Trust it is flowing where you want to go.

Look Inside

DISCOMFORT

The only behavior you can control is your own. And yet, human nature is such that when your comfort is disrupted, you seek to control the disruption rather than your response to it. There is a logic that thinks certain behaviors are unacceptable, therefore must be addressed. So, you transfer your discomfort to the offending party. Contrary to your desired outcome, the discomfort is expanded. Try another way: accept and then release your initial response. Observe the behavior that triggered your discomfort. From there, a helpful response can be initiated.

Discomfort

AMETHYST

Amethyst crystals are found inside an unremarkable gray rock. It's only when you crack it open you discover the multifaceted exquisite beauty of the deep purple majesty hidden inside. The light magnifies the treasure within. What beauty and magic is held inside you waiting to be broken open? Find it and let your crystalline nature shine.

Amethyst

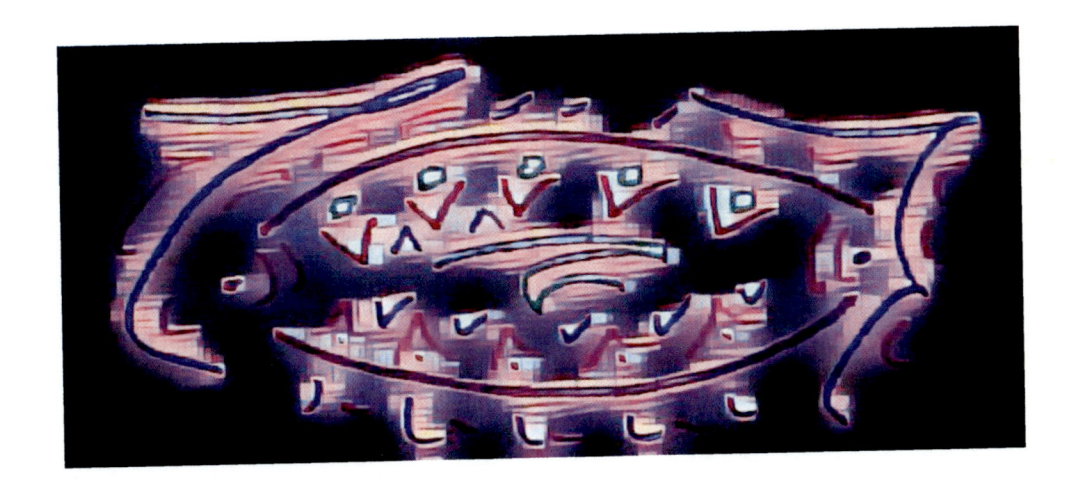

FAMILY

There is the family you're from and the family you find. Both are significant. One is your roots, the other is how you flower, forming a beautiful bouquet of purpose and meaning. And there is the human family of which you are all part. Whatever family you find yourself with today, celebrate. Celebrate you are part of something grander than your individual self. Celebrate the amazing creatures you are and what is possible to create together.

Family

DISCOVER

There's always something new to find and realize. Today, do at least three activities you haven't done before. Learn what you don't already know, not just from your computer or your phone. Take a walk somewhere you haven't been, looking along the way for what you come across. Talk to a plant and see what it has to teach you. Start a conversation with someone you don't know, opening yourself to what it might reveal. Prepare a meal you haven't yet made. Be willing to explore the unknown. Feel the enchantment from what you discover.

Discover

ROSE

The rose is an ideal metaphor for life. Its fragrant flower is intricately delicate with soft, tender petals. Below the blossom are thorns for protection that also hold the possibility to injure if not handled with care. There are phases to the rose—a sprout, a bud, a full unfolding, followed by the petals falling back to the earth to fertilize further growth. Pruning away the old, keeps the plant healthy and able to produce more flowers. This is the way of life in all its aspects. Each stage is required for growth to flourish. You are the rose. Embrace it all—the beauty and even the thorny parts.

Rose

EYES

Eyes speak the truth. Words can say all manner of mind chatter but the eyes are the pathway to the soul. Look into the eyes of another and you can see who they really are.

Eyes

RECEPTIVE

Your personal receptivity is like a radio dial. Be conscious of what you are listening too. Move past the channel of brain-chattering fear and worry. Listen instead to the sounds of nature—to the wind blowing, the crickets chirping, the flutter of butterfly wings. Then you can more easily hear the messages from Pachamama meant for you. By tuning in to the Nature Channel, it is only a small adjustment of the frequency dial to connect with Divine Source and your own inner wisdom. Be receptive.

Receptive

CHARM

Imagine you discover a charm with mystical powers in the bottom of your cup. Take it out and hold it in your palm. Examine every facet of it. Then put it in your pocket, knowing it will protect and guide you. During the day, put your hand inside and feel it with your fingertips. Know with each rub you are sending out love and light, expanding your energy field. Observe the charm and impact of your charm. Give thanks for it.

Charm

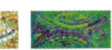

ALIGNMENT

When the planets and stars are in position, your own alignment is reflected in the heavens. Connections occur. Meetings with new people happen. Friends celebrate together. Remember you live on planet earth but you exist in a vast universe of which you are part. Alignment is happening. Feel it within you.

Alignment

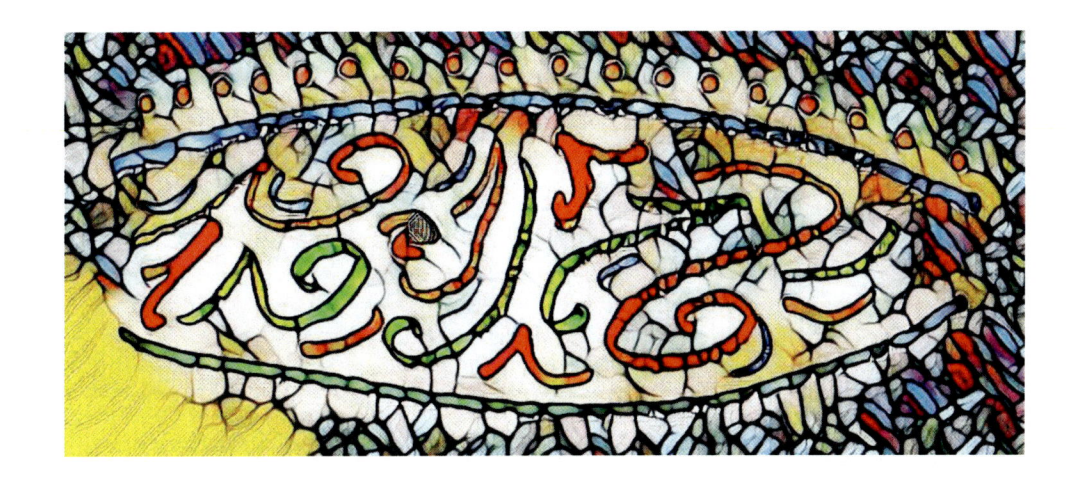

CONTRAST

For each experience of awesome joy in nature, there is an equal but opposite reaction to practical material reality, when details don't function smoothly. You can pop back into the wormhole of complaints and frustration. This and that are irritating to deal with, whereas basking in breath-taking landscape, free from outside influence, keeps you floating peacefully in the knowledge you are part of creation's perfection. The contrasts exist. Learn how to balance one with the other. That is the art of being human on planet earth.

Contrast

STABILITY

What creates stability in an unstable world is your perspective. Your personal stability comes from your feet on the ground, your heart open, your emotions balanced, your mind aware, your spirit light and trusting. You are supported by the unseen world of energy and frequency. Power structures are in flux because when systems fail to function well, they must be altered to serve the greater good. Find stability in what endures amidst all the changes, with two feet planted on the earth and love in your heart.

Stability

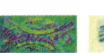

IMPLEMENT

It's time for your ideas to be implemented, to bring them to practical form. New energy is availble to you now. Use it to express yourself, drawing from the reservoir of your dreams to manifest what you want to accomplish. The universe and your soul are supporting you.

Implement

VULNERABLE

When you are in a place where you don't speak the language or even recognize the alphabet, be vulnerable. It may seem counter-intuitive, but vulnerability awakens your inner knowing and perception. By practicing this type of openness, you will recognize the value of vulnerability even when you are surrounded by the familiar.

Vulnerable

VOLUNTEER

Be proactive. Volunteer. Chose to do something that will have a positive impact on your community, your project, your life. Each small action you take creates a reaction that reverberates beyond the action itself. When you initiate something, you inspire those around you to do so as well and constructive activity begins to happen around you. Volunteer.

Volunteer

HARMONY

When there is an interweaving of difference and similarity, a community can blend to make beautiful music together. There is a congruence and balance in a unity of differences, each one contributing something unique and valuable to the whole. There is both excitement and tranquility when harmony is achieved. Seek it out. Find pleasure in it.

Harmony

EXPRESSION

To express yourself freely is a gift to be used often. The confidence to do so comes from practice. Value yourself enough to express who you are, knowing your contributions are unique. Self-expression enhances your creativity and brings joy to the child within longing to play. Let your imagination soar. Express yourself.

Expression

CALM

When something happens to disrupt your calm and serenity, there is a bio-chemical reaction in your body. Take a moment to observe what part of you is agitated. Breathe deeply, slowly. Feel your body calming itself with each slow inhale and releasing the tension with each exhale. Allow your calm centered self to resurface. Only then decide how you want to respond to the situation.

Calm

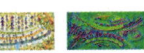

EMPOWERMENT

Humans have the capacity to choose what they think and how they respond. However, they also have subconscious programmed responses formed in childhood, often inherited from their parents. For example, when a new idea is presented to you, your automatic first response is to see all the things wrong with the idea and why it won't work. Fortunately, you have learned to recognize and bracket that response so you can see what might be beneficial in the idea and discover it's just what you've been looking for. Being conscious of old unhelpful patterns enables you to change them. That's empowerment.

Empowerment

DELIGHTFUL

Delight in surprising connections and joyful encounters. The energy rises like the moon—glowing and beautiful. Delightful experiences bring fullness to your life. Rejoice and be glad for the simple yet profound moments enabling you to feel fully alive. Delight in them.

Delightful

DISCERNMENT

There are times to be bold, to take risks and there are times to surrender your will to what is presented, even when it is not to your liking. It takes discernment to know when to do which. Attention to your inner wisdom should be given and trusted. By releasing the need to control outside circumstances, you can use whatever is happening to your advantage. The choice is yours.

Discernment

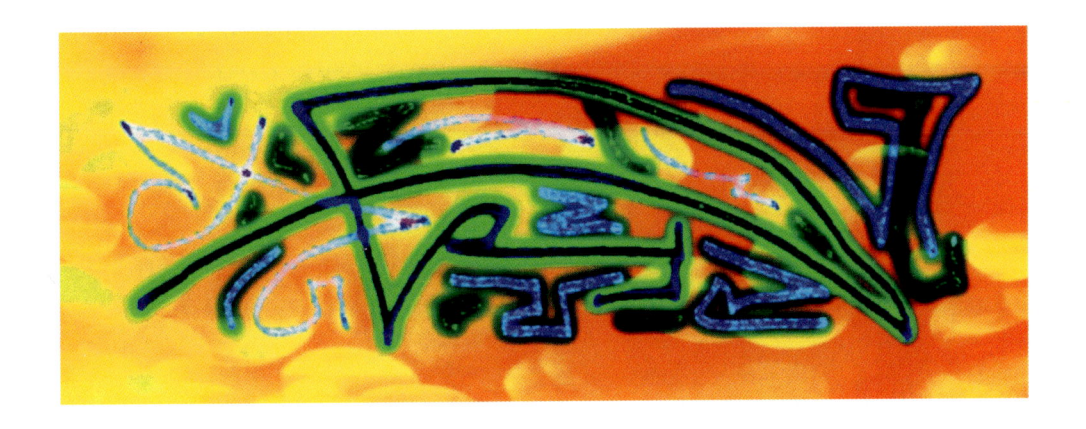

INDEX OF PEARLS

Adapt 134	Discomfort 170	Momentum 32	Soft Spot 28
Alchemy 138	Discover 176	Mystery 8	Stability 190
Alignment 186	Divine Spark 110	Notice 162	Stars 78
Allow 120	Ease 96	Nourishment 48	Stillness 30
Amethyst 172	Empowerment 204	Orientation 58	Strength 122
Aware 50	Enthusiasm 56	Passenger 20	Surrender 144
Befriend 130	Equilibrium 12	Peace 40	Sustenance 72
Be Nimble 114	Expression 200	Pearls 26	Symphony 104
Birth 44	Express Yourself 126	Pearls & Codes 1	Synchronicity 124
Bridge 60	Eyes 180	Perspective 10	Tapestry 36
Bright Side 80	Faith 14	Play 136	Thrive 88
Calm 202	Family 174	Pot Luck 102	Transformation 92
Capable 112	Flexible 106	Preparation 98	Traveler of Light 166
Centered 42	Free 70	Pyramid 46	Treasure Chest 164
Change 4	Grace 2	Ready 90	Triggers 54
Charm 184	Hands 146	Receive 82	Trust 68
Compassion 154	Harmony 198	Receptive 182	Truth 18
Consider 150	Implement 192	Refresh 132	Turtle & Eagle 148
Container 108	Innovate 22	Relinquish Control 118	Unexpected 158
Content 140	Integrity 74	Research 84	Volunteer 196
Contents v	In The Moment 128	Reunion 142	Vulnerable 194
Contrast 188	Introduction vii	Risk 100	Wait 38
Create 66	Listening 6	Roots 86	Waves 152
Dance 76	Look Inside 168	Rose 178	Wellspring 52
Delightful 206	Love 34	Sacred Center 116	Willingness 16
Departure 64	Magic 94	Sense of Humor 24	Wisdom 156
Discernment 208	Meantime 160	Signals 62	

ABOUT THE AUTHOR

Originally from New York, Diane Dunn had a career in theatre before she felt her first call toward a life of Spirit. She entered Union Theological Seminary and graduated with a Masters of Divinity. In the 1990s, just after the liberation of Nelson Mandela, she worked in South Africa where she developed an outreach program for the homeless in Johannesburg. It was there she was introduced to Peruvian shamanism and was inspired by her teacher's vision of a spiritual center in Cusco's Sacred Valley.

She moved to Peru without knowing the country, the language, or how she would support herself, but a deep trust she was on the right path kept her moving magically toward greater adventures and greater understanding of how Spirit was at work in her life. She built a house, a few guest rooms, more guest rooms, a conference room, a restaurant and a spa, then realized she had created the spiritual center of her teacher's vision one small step at a time.

It was there she met her soulmate, Christer, in another moment of magic, only to have him die suddenly after a few short years together. Again, her connection to Spirit transformed that experience into something profound and beautiful.

In the twenty-plus years she has lived in Peru, the world has changed dramatically. What has not changed is her commitment to be a conduit of love and peace for humanity and the planet.

This is her fourth book. Find out more about Diane, her work, and her life on her website: *www.dianedunn.net*.

Made in United States
Orlando, FL
26 July 2024